YOU CHOSE BRUCE

CHIC
SIMPLE ™
Components

DURANTE: "Hey, where are my glasses?"

FRIEND: "They're on your nose!"

DURANTE: "Be more specific!"

JIMMY DURANTE

CHIC
SIMPLE™
Components

SPECTACLES

THAMES AND HUDSON

FIRST PUBLISHED IN GREAT BRITAIN IN 1994
BY THAMES AND HUDSON LTD, LONDON

KIM JOHNSON GROSS   JEFF STONE

WRITTEN BY MICHAEL SOLOMON
PHOTOGRAPHS BY JAMES WOJCIK
STYLED BY JEFFREY MILLER

DESIGN AND ART DIRECTION BY
ROBERT VALENTINE INCORPORATED
ILLUSTRATIONS BY GREGG NEMEC
ICON ILLUSTRATION BY ERIC HANSON

British Library Cataloguing-in-Publication Data
A catalogue record for this book is available from the British Library

ISBN 0-500-01618-6

Printed in Canada

CONTENTS

SPECTACLES

*A history of the eyepiece, corrective and protective eyewear,
materials, a perfect fit, and identity*

11

ANATOMY

Lenses, coatings, tintings, sunglasses, frames, and cases

27

A VISUAL LEXICON

*Reading glasses, bifocals, trifocals, folding glasses, wire rims,
tortoiseshell, horn-rims, and metal frames*

41

SPORT GLASSES

*Classic sunglasses, mirrored lenses, water sports, beach sports,
mountain sports, shooting, and other specialty eyewear*

65

FIRST AID

*Eye doctors, the eye chart, children's vision and eyewear, and
shopping for glasses*

80

WHERE

Worldwide guide: retail, outlets, catalogues

84

"The more you know, the less you need."

AUSTRALIAN ABORIGINAL SAYING

CHIC
SIMPLE ™

Chic Simple is a primer for living well but sensibly. It's for those who believe that quality of life does not come in accumulating things, but in paring down to the essentials. Chic Simple enables readers to bring value and style into their lives with economy and simplicity.

S P E C T A C L E S

They are the difference between Clark Kent and Superman.
They make us look smarter. And nerdier. And sometimes
even sexier. They are signs that we are getting old. Or
pretentious. They make the world come into focus and
they keep us from being seen. They are storm windows for
our windows to the soul. But the most important thing
about spectacles is remembering where you left them last.

"People see only what they are
prepared to see."

RALPH WALDO EMERSON

THE HISTORY OF THE EYEPIECE
IS A BIT FUZZY, BUT IT SEEMS THAT

SPECTACLES WERE MOST LIKELY INVENTED SIMULTANEOUSLY during the late 13th century in Italy and China. Because few people could read or owned books, and because glasses were so expensive, wearing them was a symbol of wisdom and wealth. Some 14th-century aristocrats wore them without lenses simply to appear more intelligent. The earliest lenses were made of glass or transparent stones, and since they were convex, they were only useful to farsighted people, to help with reading and close vision. Concave lenses, for nearsighted people, were not invented until the early 15th century. It was not until the mid-17th century that spectacles with rigid temples were introduced —which meant they finally stopped sliding off the nose.

"I have eyes like those of a dead pig."

MARLON BRANDO

13TH CENTURY *Friar Roger Bacon, a Franciscan monk, was imprisoned for heresy in the late thirteenth century for writing about the merits of spectacles.* **17TH CENTURY** *Marie Antoinette made lorgnette glasses, which had a handle and were held in front of the eyes, fashionable. Spectacles came over to America on the* Mayflower *in 1620 with passenger Peter Brown.* **18TH CENTURY** *In the late eighteenth century, George Washington bought a pair of imported spectacles with engraved silver frames for $75, an astronomical amount for the time.* **19TH CENTURY** *When Abraham Lincoln purchased his first pair of spectacles in the 1860s, he paid 37 cents.* **20TH CENTURY** *Despite his bland reputation, Harry Truman wore three different styles of frame while in office.*

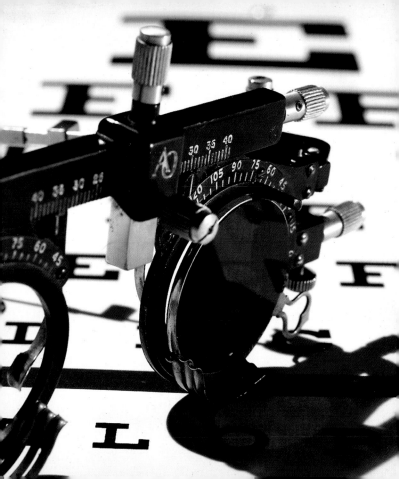

Corrective. Several serious health risks can cause or contribute to eye problems—diabetes, hardening of the arteries, even high blood pressure—but essentially there are four types of refractive errors that can be corrected with spectacles. With **MYOPIA**, or nearsightedness, individuals can see objects better up close than far away. While many are born nearsighted, myopia often arises during the pre-teen or teen years. A relatively new surgical procedure known as radial keratotomy, or RK, helps correct myopia, but its long-term effects are still unknown. **HYPEROPIA**, or farsightedness, affects close vision, but not distances, and tends to develop during the teens or the twenties. **ASTIGMATISM** is a condition that causes a distortion of image and blurs vision in one direction. And, finally, as we age, the eye gradually loses its ability to focus on close objects—which is why people start holding books in the next zip code to read them. This condition, known as **PRESBYOPIA**, usually occurs after forty and affects more than seventy-five million Americans.

Protective. Think back to childhood. You're horsing around with some friends when suddenly your mother barks, "Stop that or somebody's going to lose an eye." Sure it was annoying to hear, but you stopped—for about a minute, and then you giggled and pretended that your eye fell out. The truth is, of course, that eyes do need protection—from the sun, small objects, and the occasional elbow. And whether you work with dangerous machinery, play a lot of racquet sports, or spend a lot of time outdoors, there are protective glasses and lenses to suit your needs. In other words, once again, your mother was right.

WORK

Nearly 60 percent of eye injuries in the workplace happen to people not wearing eye protection. And while computer screens aren't as dangerous as, say, radial saws, they can be a tremendous strain on the eyes. Occasionally looking away from the screen helps.

SPORTS

One of the basic rules in sports is to keep your eye on the ball, but when it's travelling at more than 100 miles per hour—as squash balls, tennis balls, and baseballs are wont to do—it becomes quite a treacherous concept.

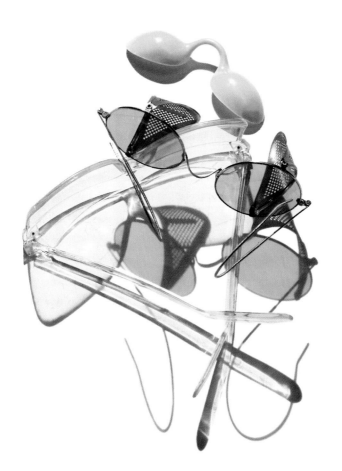

Material. One of the reasons the earliest glasses were so expensive was that they used the most luxurious materials—bone, horn, tortoiseshell, and ivory for the frames. The major downside of this, however, was that when combined with glass lenses, the glasses were so heavy they tended to cause a lot of headaches. It wasn't until the introduction of plastic frames and lenses (in the early twentieth century) that wearing glasses all day long became possible. Plastic and wire frames with plastic lenses can still feel a bit hefty, so lighter materials for the frames, and thinner lenses, are being used to help take a great weight off your nose and ears.

THE LIGHT BRIGADE *Traditionally, the choice was between metal and plastic. And life was simple: if the prescription was high-powered (meaning the lens would be heavy), then plastic was called for. Not so today. With all the advances in technology there are now lightweight metals such as stainless steel and even ultra-lightweight (but incredibly sturdy) materials such as titanium. Plastic frames are now being made out of lightweight nylon. And there are also carbon fiber (or graphite) frames that are strong and lightweight.*

Fit. Anyone who's ever had the full-scale panic of sitting on a pair of glasses knows how important (and fragile) fit is. And as with any custom-made item, there's no reason to sacrifice comfort for style. The first concern when fitting glasses is to make sure the centers of the lenses are directly in line with the pupils; a skilled optician or optometrist should be able to insure proper placement by adjusting the nose pads. The next parts to consider are the temple pieces; they shouldn't touch the head until they reach the ears. Also, make sure the temples sit above or below the pupils and do not obstruct peripheral vision. The Big Picture: oversize frames may look better on some faces, but keep in mind that they require bigger lenses, which may add weight to the glasses as well as distort vision.

"I have such poor vision I can date anybody."

GARRY SHANDLING

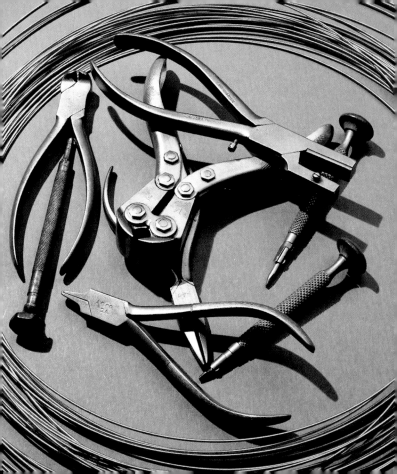

MODERN CAT'S-EYE GLASSES

Aluminum Frame with Plastic Arms

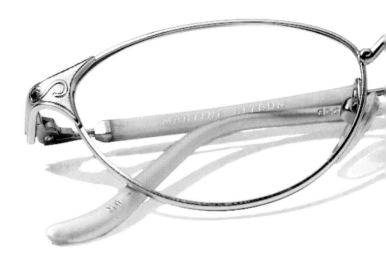

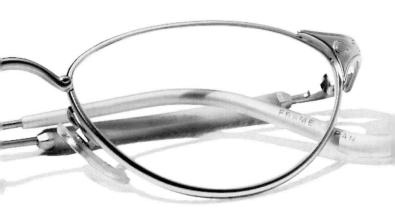

STYLE

*Spectacles make a personal statement but there's no reason they have
to shout. Sometimes the boldest approach to wearing glasses is a simple, clean
design. (It will lighten the load on your nose, but perhaps not your wallet.)
Because as with many things, less is often more.*

"A celebrity is a person who works hard all his life to become well known, then wears dark glasses to avoid being recognized."

FRED ALLEN

Keith Haring *Cary Grant* Woody Allen
Henry Kissinger Yves Saint-Laurent *Spike Lee* Buddy Holly *Allen Ginsberg*
Le Corbusier *Philip Johnson* Clark Kent *Garth*

Identity. Dorothy Parker scared off a generation of women from wearing glasses with her wicked words: "Men seldom make passes at girls who wear glasses." But glasses can also create a positive identity. Imagine the late Swifty Lazar without his trademark black windshields. Or Sally Jessy Raphael without her oversized red frames. Or Jack Nicholson sitting courtside without his shades. For some, glasses are more defining than facial features, proving that beauty is often lens deep.

Roy Orbison *Tom Cruise*
Don Johnson *The Blues Brothers*
Jack Nicholson

Daryl Hannah *Marlee Matlin*
Selma Diamond *Sophia Loren*
Dame Edna Everage

Groucho Marx *Ernest Hemingway*
Theodore Roosevelt *William Hurt*
John Lennon *Mahatma Gandhi*
Joseph Stalin *David Letterman*
Whoopi Goldberg

James Dean Harold Lloyd
T. S. Eliot Jodie Foster
Jean-Paul Sartre

My Family Helps Me Breathe (handwritten)

A N A T O M Y

Whether they are a fashion accessory or the only thing keeping you from stumbling blindly through life, glasses are an investment and you should know what you're paying for. Besides the initial cost of frames, there are always additional expenses, such as extra-thin lenses, their tintings and coatings, which can quickly add up. So keep your eyes open.

"Vision is the art of seeing things invisible."

JONATHAN SWIFT

Lenses. Plastic lenses—with their dual qualities of lightness and impact resistance—have largely replaced glass but often need a scratch-resistant coating. Other options for lenses include UV, or ultraviolet, coatings to filter the harmful rays of the sun, although most lenses already offer adequate UV protection; tinting, or gradient tinting, to bring some relief (but no extra protection) from the sun; photochromic lenses, which lighten or darken depending on the amount of sunlight; and anti-reflective coatings, which eliminate glare and shine on the lens.

BIFOCALS *They allow you to see near and far with one lens. Some people think of the bifocal "lines" like wrinkles and would rather not see than admit to growing older.* TRIFOCALS *While bifocals take care of near and far, they ignore middle distances. Trifocals offer distance vision at the top of the lens, medium distance in the middle, and close distance at the bottom. The jump in vision may take getting used to.* PROGRESSIVE LENSES *These are essentially "hidden-line" bifocals and trifocals that offer a smooth, gradual transition between the ranges of vision. It may take a while to master the different sections, and they cost about twice as much as conventional bifocals.*

Shades. Except when they're worn at the Academy Awards, sunglasses are an essential part of protection from the sun. As with any sun protection, there are three types of ultraviolet rays to beware of—UVA, which may or may not be harmful, but why take chances; UVB, which cause cataracts and other eye diseases; and UVC, which is cancer causing but blocked by what's left of the ozone layer. The tint of the glasses will block the visible light (but not the UV rays) and you can check this by trying on the glasses and looking in the mirror: if you can see your eyes they're too light. Another good test for sunglasses is to look at a traffic light. If you can't tell the colors apart, stop. Try a different tint. Wraparound sunglasses—which are seemingly the best defense from the rays— have their own problems: the curve of the lens creates distortion, except on such high-tech models as Oakley and Gargoyle. Believe it or not, some ten-dollar sunglasses can offer adequate protection.

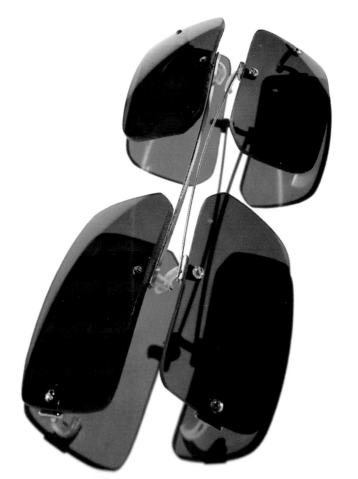

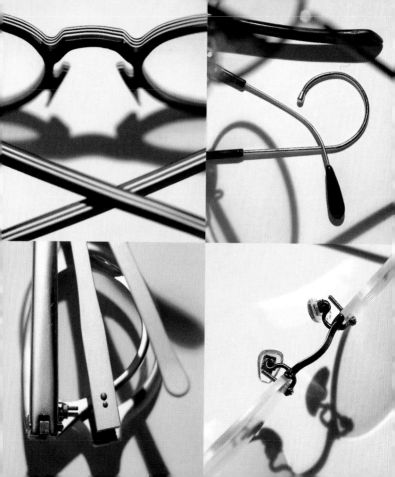

Frames. The frame should relate to the distance between the temples, as well as bone structure. **BRIDGE.** The bridge should be neither too loose nor too tight (which might affect breathing). **NOSE PADS.** If the glasses are not uni-body, they will have nose pads, which will affect how heavy they feel on the nose. Silicon pads are more comfortable than hard plastic and easy to clean. **HINGES.** Hinges should be made of metal, not plastic, and have real screws rather than pins. Spring hinges on the temples will keep the sides from bowing, which means you can stop panicking when people with enormous heads try on your glasses.

TEMPLES

There are three types from which to choose:

STANDARD
which have a slight bend

LIBRARY
which are straight

CABLE
which curve behind the ear.

No matter what style you select, the sides should swing smoothly.

Simple Glasses. Of all the thousands of styles of spectacles, none is as simple as the Ben Franklin or granny glasses—rimless lenses with wire temple pieces. Just about the only thing to experiment with is the shape of the lens itself—octagonal, rectangular, or the simplest choice, round. With their wraparound ear pieces, rimless glasses connote a certain hard-core bookishness, as though they are never going to be taken off. The stark design—and you really can't get more utilitarian than two pieces of wire and some glass—reflects a certain austerity. And perhaps best of all, they all but disappear on the face.

"He came up to my table.... He took my glasses off and he said, 'Without your glasses, why, you're beautiful.' I said, 'Without my glasses, you're not half bad either.'"

KIT HOLLERBACH

SIMPLE
SUNGLASSES

Clip-on sunglasses were first introduced in the early twentieth century, but they never really caught on—they were considered eccentric and, for some odd reason, impractical— until they were re-introduced in the early Eighties by l.a. Eyeworks. Today, of course, they are an ideal choice for sunglasses. They're cheaper than a full pair of prescription sunglasses because there is less material. They maintain the design purity of the frame and they're relatively hassle-free. Just clip them on and go.

On the Case. Most glasses take so much punishment in everyday use that they deserve a rest from time to time. If you're just taking them off for a moment, place them carefully—with the bridge down or with the lenses up. Never put your lenses on a hard surface. If you're putting your glasses away for a while, keep them in a case, ideally a hard one. A soft case, while offering protection for the lenses, won't make a bit of difference if you sit on them. And a floating case will help prevent a sea of troubles. Cases can also make a style statement—like luggage for spectacles—and antique cases, especially those that are bejeweled, are even collected.

CLEANING YOUR GLASSES

1. Take them off your face.
2. Hold them by the bridge.
3. Carefully wipe the lenses with warm water and soap (glass cleaner can damage the frame), rinse, then dry with a tissue or soft cloth.
4. Never clean your glasses when they're dry—unless you have a specially treated lens cloth, such as Luminex—this is how small scratches are made.

A VISUAL LEXICON

Sometimes it seems as if there are more shapes, colors, and styles for spectacles than there are eyes. Even looking for the simplest pair of glasses can take hours—if not days. So it's wise to know what you're looking for.

"I wear eyeglasses during the day. The other day I was walking down the street and my prescription ran out."

STEVEN WRIGHT

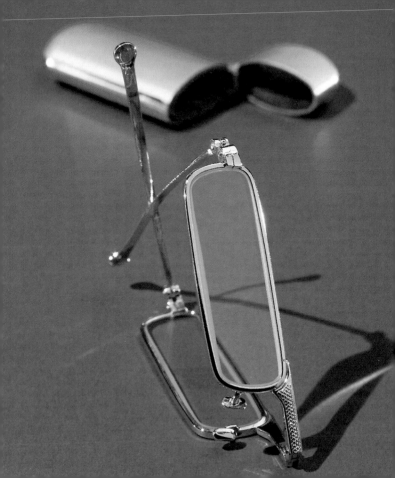

Reading Glasses. The first stage of coping with reading glasses is denial. The second is the headaches from the first. No one wants to admit that the years are creeping up. But there's no shame in admitting you're having trouble with the fine print. In fact, it's just plain foolish to put off a proper eye exam. Some people may opt for full reading lenses, but many prefer half-lenses—especially those who are farsighted and like to see distances when they look up. Of course, reading glasses can also be a fashion choice (attorney William Kunstler, for example, always wears his on his forehead). They instantly give that avuncular look.

FOLDING GLASSES

Reading glasses don't take up that much room to begin with, but a folding pair is even more economical—at least as far as space is concerned. The only downside is, when glasses are that compact, it may be even harder to find them than normal.

MYTH INFORMATION

You cannot "wear your eyes out." Reading in poor light will not ruin them or worsen a pre-existing eye condition. Low light will, however, tire the eyes more quickly than good lighting.

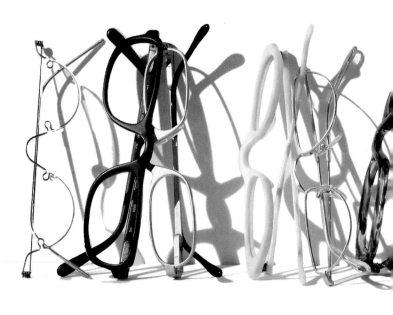

ON THE TIP OF YOUR NOSE *Reading glasses are not just for grandparents anymore. With all of the high-tech materials and stylish designs— such as folding glasses or half-sunglasses—they are ideal for anyone regardless of age. And if an eye doctor doesn't find anything too serious, non-prescription*

glasses (like the kind you find in the drugstore for about ten dollars) are often good enough. These inexpensive reading glasses work like a magnifying glass and come in a variety of powers. Buying several pairs of these cheap reading glasses is also the best way to combat the eternal problem of losing them.

WIRE RIM

THERE WAS A TIME WHEN THESE GLASSES WERE ONLY MADE WITH WIRE, BUT TODAY YOU ARE more likely to find a pair made with a sturdy but malleable metal. Because wire rims are delicate, they are probably best suited to a prescription that is not too strong—otherwise the lenses pop out. Wire rim glasses come in just about every shade of metal so there should be a pair that's right for your skin tone and hair color. (A current popular style is a hybrid of wire rims with a tortoiseshell coating.) In general, though, gold, copper, and bronze frames are best suited for blondes, redheads, and people with brown hair, while silver, chrome, or black wire rims look best on those with black, gray, or silver hair. One of the charms of wire rims is that they are light, and can take a lot of punishment and still fit perfectly. Which means that you don't have to get bent out of shape if they do.

"The farther back
you can look, the
farther forward you
are likely to see."

WINSTON CHURCHILL

TORTOISESHELL

BECAUSE THE CHINESE CONSIDERED THE TORTOISE SACRED, WEARING TORTOISESHELL GLASSES WAS thought to bring good luck. (In fact, they used the material for many decorative objects.) The Spanish, however, simply considered it high fashion. So high that in 1701, when King Philip V and his wife María Luisa of Savoy arrived in Madrid, her five hundred ladies-in-waiting were all wearing tortoiseshell frames. When tortoiseshell was actually made from the shell, the material was so thin that several pieces had to be liquefied and molded together. Today, tortoiseshell frames are almost certainly made of plastic, but this preppy favorite endures because it is flattering on just about any face. The traditional dark, mottled brown works best on brunettes, while the lighter browns are more suited for blondes. There are even frivolous tortoiseshell colors—red, blue, green—confirming that today nothing is sacred.

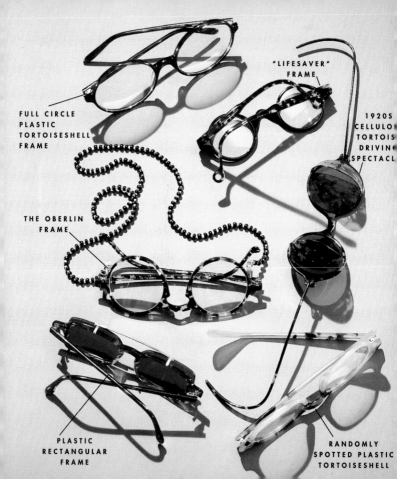

FULL CIRCLE
PLASTIC
TORTOISESHELL
FRAME

"LIFESAVER"
FRAME

1920S
CELLULO
TORTOIS
DRIVIN
SPECTACL

THE OBERLIN
FRAME

PLASTIC
RECTANGULAR
FRAME

RANDOMLY
SPOTTED PLASTIC
TORTOISESHELL

PLASTIC TORTOISE
SPECTACLES CASE

CAT'S-EYE
SUNGLASSES

VINTAGE CHILD'S
FRAME

OVAL PLASTIC
TORTOISE FRAME

VINTAGE PLASTIC
TORTOISE "OWL-
EYES"

HANDMADE
"LIGHT"
TORTOISE

SEPTILATERAL
PLASTIC TORTOISE
FRAME

HORN RIM

LIKE JUST ABOUT EVERY OLD-FASHIONED FRAME MATERIAL, THE NAME HORN RIM IS ACTUALLY A misnomer. At one time animals' horns were used to make frames. Now these frames are plastic. The thick and usually black frames we think of as horn-rims have an almost comic, nerdy air to them, enabling them to transform any fashion model into a librarian, any leading man into an absentminded professor. Perhaps the most recognizable style of horn-rims is the round frame, worn by Philip Johnson and I. M. Pei, guys who know something about design.

"For more serious occasions, put your horn-rim glasses in your breast pocket, leaving one earpiece hanging outside your coat. This reminds others that you may have to read an important telex or vital deal memo at any moment—very smart looking."

P. J. O'ROURKE

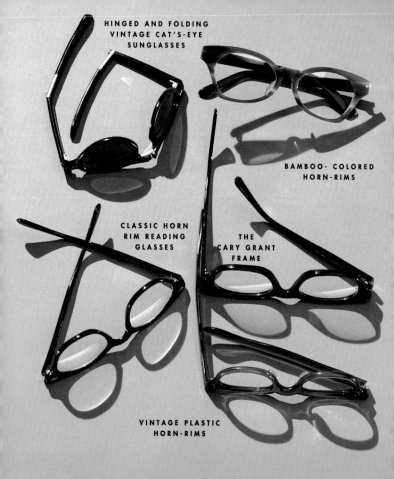

HINGED AND FOLDING
VINTAGE CAT'S-EYE
SUNGLASSES

BAMBOO- COLORED
HORN-RIMS

CLASSIC HORN
RIM READING
GLASSES

THE
CARY GRANT
FRAME

VINTAGE PLASTIC
HORN-RIMS

CLASSIC
HORN-RIMS

"SECRET AGENT"
SUNGLASSES

HAND-HELD
LORGNETTE

ROUND BLACK
"CORBUSIER"
FRAME

Shape. Spectacles should complement facial features. In general, the frame should be about as wide as the widest part of the face—try something a little wider for a narrow face and bit narrower for a wide face. The size of the frames should reflect bone structure and features: that is, large frames for large features and vice versa. Frames should also counterbalance facial structure. If you have a round face, for example, choose something angular, and avoid something too round or too square. To shorten a long nose, find glasses with a low or dark-colored bridge. However, beware of aviator frames as you get older; they're not very kind when it comes to gravity.

Color. Like shape, the color of the frames should reflect your features. Choosing frames that are no darker than your hair color is a safe rule, but sometimes very dark frames are more striking. If you are very pale, select a frame that brings a little color to your face—and get a pair of sunglasses so you can get outside more.

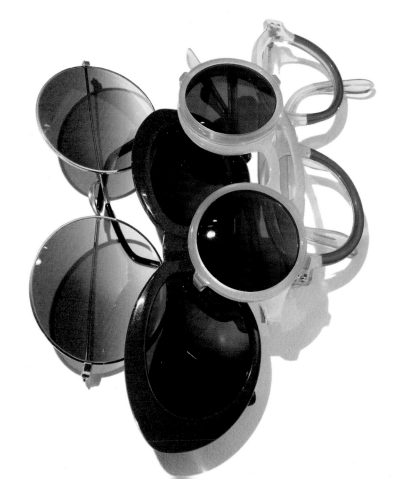

Sun Tints. Assuming that your sunglasses provide adequate protection, the next consideration is tinting. Gray is the most versatile tint and provides the truest perception of color. Green lenses also provide great clarity and block dangerous blue light. Brown lenses also block blue light and are good for cutting through haze.

Cosmetic Tints. If you're not looking for sun protection, but just want to look at the world through, say, rose-colored glasses, cosmetic tinting is just the answer. Try not to get something too dark and be aware that blue lenses, while wonderfully psychedelic, can make it difficult to discern colors. Custom tinting (usually amber, but it depends on your screen color) can also be useful for someone who stares at a computer all day.

Metal. Because glasses were first worn by the wealthy, some of the earliest materials used in them were, naturally, luxurious—gold and silver. Later, as wearing glasses became more widespread, light steel and wire were very fashionable—and certainly cheaper. As technology advanced in this century, lighter metals —such as nickel in the Twenties, aluminum in the Sixties and Seventies—proved popular. Today, metal frames, especially titanium, are enjoying a renaissance (particularly in sunglasses) because they're durable and reflect a certain asceticism—despite the price tag. Just as with plastic frames, the same rules apply when choosing metal frame color: follow hair color and skin tones.

"Your Eyes Match Garbo's, Baby, I Wish They Matched Each Other."

HENRY MORGAN

SPORT GLASSES

Just as you would never go skiing without the right
bindings or go fly-fishing without hip waders, you
should never ignore the importance of spectacles.
Indeed, choosing a good pair of glasses can be the
most important equipment decision you make.

"Save your breath, you may want it
to clean your glasses later."

JULES TANNEN

Classics

In 1930, Bausch & Lomb created
a pair of sunglasses to help United
States Army pilots see through
the glare at high altitudes—
green lenses in aviator goggles.

WRAPAROUND
*sunglasses may be the coolest
Ray-Ban style of all, but it takes a
certain facial shape, not to mention
personality, to carry them off.
Dirty Harry, for instance.*

AVIATOR
*frames became the trademark for
Douglas MacArthur, though still
not standard issue.*

WAYFARER

sunglasses were introduced in the 1950s and never really caught on until Tom Cruise peered out from under a pair in Risky Business *and Don Johnson looked for drug dealers in them on* Miami Vice.

MILITARY

style sunglasses are close cousins of aviators—a little more rectangular, and a little more retro, though no less classic. Like aviators, they convey a certain amount of authority.

"I never wore sunglasses until a few years ago—I felt I had enough attitude as it was."

FRAN LEBOWITZ

Mirrored. Could there be a more anti-social style of sunglasses than ones with mirrored lenses? Put them on and suddenly the rest of the world is in your own private interrogation room—you can look out at it, but it can't look in on you. In fact, the notion of hiding one's eyes goes back to the origin of sunglasses themselves, when Chinese judges put smoke-colored quartz in front of their eyes so their verdicts could not be anticipated. Which is perhaps why many highway patrolmen prefer mirrored sunglasses: you can't tell if your pitiful story is affecting them or not. In addition to being an instant compact for quick lipstick checks, mirrored sunglasses are very practical. Because they block glare so well, they are ideal for snow sports. (Mirrored lenses scratch easily, however, and cannot be treated with a scratch-resistant coating.) And mirrored lenses are no longer made in just that silver tint. Today, companies such as Revo and Vuarnet, among others, make mirrored lenses in nearly every color of the spectrum.

Sport Glasses. There are glasses for every sport imaginable. Need a pair for climbing? Cycling? Windsurfing? They're out there. There are two things to consider when buying eyewear for sports— vision enhancement and safety. **WATER SPORTS.** Photochromic lenses are very effective, as are polarized lenses, which eliminate reflected glare and allow you to see a foot or two in the water. **BEACH SPORTS.** Like glasses for water sports, beach sports also require glasses that cut glare. Sunglasses such as Gargoyles, Bollé, and Oakleys are ideal for volleyball or windsurfing because they are lightweight, aerodynamic, and highly impact-resistant. **SHOOTING.** Amber- or vermilion-colored glasses are the best choice for shooting; they allow for the greatest clarity under flat light conditions.

> " I never questioned the integrity of an umpire.
> Their eyesight, yes."
>
> LEO DUROCHER

AERODYNAMIC
*Hi-tech wraparound
glasses are more than just
a fashion statement—
they're aerodynamic
necessities
in sports such as cycling,
where every hundredth of
a second counts.
Wraparound sunglasses
are also great for
volleyball because they
block the sun and the
sand.*

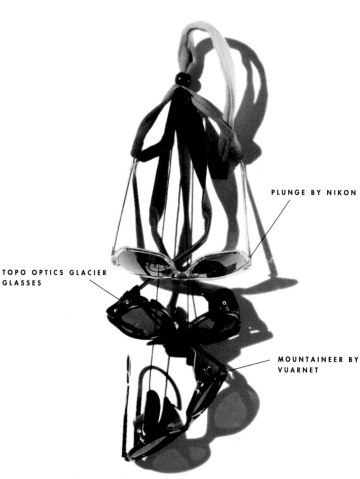

PLUNGE BY NIKON

TOPO OPTICS GLACIER GLASSES

MOUNTAINEER BY VUARNET

Mountain Sports. Because the air is thinner, the sun is stronger, extra protection is needed. Yellow or amber lenses give the best resolution. Serengeti, Vuarnet, REI, or EMS make a variety of glasses for climbing, complete with nose and side shields. But don't use them while skiing, as they block peripheral vision. For downhill skiing, sunglasses have been replaced by goggles—usually yellow or rose-colored —which also work in white-out conditions. Goggles can also be made with your prescription. But for cross-country trekking, whether by skis or snowshoes, mountain glasses are great both for glare or flat light.

IN A FOG? You don't have to get all steamed up every time you enter the ski lodge. There are many anti-fog products—coated, microfine cloths—which will take care of any unwanted condensation.

VUARNET *In 1951, Pouilloux, a French company, created the Skilynx lens to provide clear vision under all weather conditions. The glasses proved very popular with sportsmen, including the French ski champion Jean Vuarnet, under whose surname Pouilloux sunglasses are now sold.*

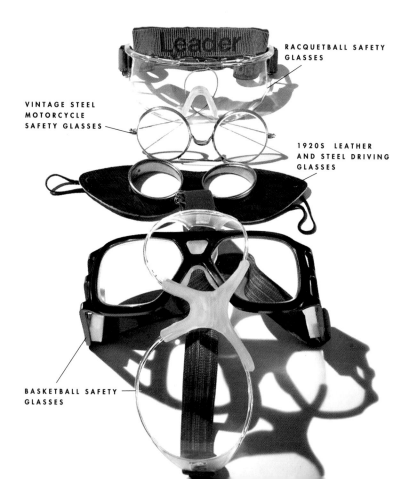

RACQUETBALL SAFETY GLASSES

VINTAGE STEEL MOTORCYCLE SAFETY GLASSES

1920S LEATHER AND STEEL DRIVING GLASSES

BASKETBALL SAFETY GLASSES

Protective. Whether you are at work or at play, protective eyewear can mean the difference between a serious scare and serious injury. Don't be fooled because you're wearing your regular spectacles; they can shatter and cause great damage. Consider wearing safety goggles over them, or better yet, have the prescription put into the safety lenses. Safety lenses should be made of polycarbonate, which is incredibly impact-resistant. The frames should be impact-resistant as well and made of plastic, rubber, or nylon. For sports, the glasses should not have molded hinges at the temple as these can be dangerous.

CROAKIES

Skiing down a mountain can be difficult enough without having to worry about keeping your glasses on. In 1976, Robbie Fuller, a Jackson Hole, Wyoming, ski patrolman, cut a few strips of neoprene from a wet suit and made adjustable straps to hold his glasses in place. He called his invention "croakies," a ski patrol expression for whatchamacallit. Today, eyeglass straps are popular among skiers, professional athletes, or anyone who's just a little too active.

Specialty. An amazing number of eyewear options are available. And if the glasses you want don't already exist, chances are that a skilled optician or a company that handles special orders can make it for you. Want a pair of goggles with adjustable lenses for light and dark water? No problem. Afraid to wear your contacts with a scuba mask or goggles? Simple. Just have the prescription ground right into them. Or how about that infuriating tendency to lose your glasses while wading in the ocean? Never again. Many companies make glasses that float so nearsighted water-skiers and surfers can now feel safe. The point is that—for a price—you can have glasses made that take into account all of your personal quirks and passions.

SAFETY GLASSES AND GOGGLES STANDARDS *For sports, glasses should meet the American Society for Testing and Material standard ASTM F.803. For industrial use, glasses should have the seal of the American National Standards Institute, ANSI Z87.1. Some companies—Gargoyle and Oakley—even boast that their lenses can stop bullets.*

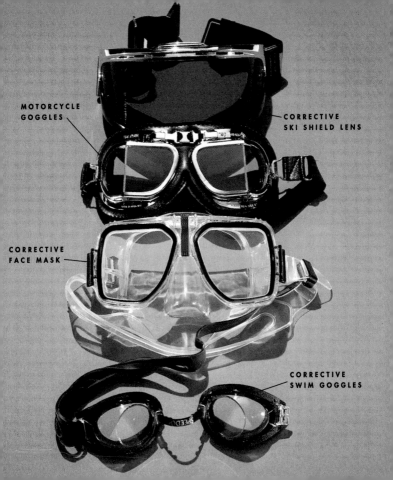

MOTORCYCLE
GOGGLES

CORRECTIVE
SKI SHIELD LENS

CORRECTIVE
FACE MASK

CORRECTIVE
SWIM GOGGLES

# first aid. You'll sit on
them, misplace them, or just get tired of seeing yourself in them. So it's
wise to know how to take care of your glasses and, of course, your eyes.

THE FIRST STEP TO WEARING

glasses is having your eyes checked regularly. The American Optometric Association offers the following recommendations for eye exams:

- *pre-school to twenty-five: yearly.*
- *twenty-five to thirty-five: every two years*
- *thirty-five and over: yearly*

20/20 EXPLAINED

The term 20/20 is based on the Snellen eye chart. Created in 1863 by Herman Snellen, the chart features letters (or symbols for children and people who cannot discern letters) and is placed twenty feet away from the viewer. The vision score is determined by the last line of the chart you are able to read.

For example, a score of 20/40 means that you were able to read from twenty feet what a person with normal vision could read from forty feet away. In other words, your vision is

below normal. A score of 20/15 means that you can read at twenty feet what a person with normal vision could read only by moving up five feet. Therefore, your vision is better than normal. And 20/20? It means your vision is normal—no better, no worse.

LEARNING THE O'S

OPHTHALMOLOGIST
A medical doctor who can examine your eyes, diagnose diseases, prescribe glasses and contact lenses (and occasionally even sell them), and perform eye surgery.

OPTOMETRIST
An eye specialist who performs examinations, detects eye diseases, and prescribes and dispenses glasses. Some, but not all, states allow optometrists to prescribe eye medication.

OPTICIAN
A technician who grinds lenses, and makes, fits, and dispenses glasses. An optician cannot examine eyes or write prescriptions.

OPTIMIST

Someone who believes his eyesight will never go bad.

A BIRD'S-EYE VIEW

Eagles have long been famous for their acute vision because of their superb hunting skills. And like most predators, or reasonably intelligent creatures—most notably man— their eyes are in the front of their head, which is vital to keen sight.

EVER SEE A RABBIT WITH GLASSES?

Carrots really do improve vision. The vitamin A in carrots and other yellow, orange, and dark green vegetables is essential for maintaining normal vision and is especially key for night vision.

MYTH INFORMATION

Watching too much television will not damage the eyes, and sitting too close isn't so terrible either. In fact, sitting too faraway from the TV may make it difficult to see.

CHILDREN'S VISION

One of the biggest problems with determining if a child has vision problems is that he is unlikely to speak up about it. So here are some signs to watch out for:

- *holding objects especially close*
- *excessive rubbing, blinking or squinting of the eyes*
- *tilting the head to one side*
- *moving the head (and not the eyes) when reading*
- *constant letter or word reversal after the age of seven*
- *headaches after reading*
- *red or watery eyes (which could also be a sign of allergies)*
- *poor hand-eye coordination (though this may reflect muscle problems, not vision problems)*

CHILDREN'S GLASSES

If a vision problem is detected and children do require glasses, here are some helpful hints:

- *choose glasses with cable temples that wrap around the ear so they can't come off easily*
- *durable, malleable metals and hard plastics are likely to withstand all the punishment a kid can muster*
- *lightweight eyewear is best for children because heavier glasses often leave red marks on the nose, which is still soft and growing*
- *bright, colorful frames are especially popular with children. Why make them look like young fogeys?*

ANATOMY OF THE LENS

(Average charges)

Basic plastic or glass lenses: $50–75

High-index (or very thin) lenses: $100–150

Scratch-resistant coating: $20

UV coating: $20–25

Tinting: $15–20

Anti-reflective coating: $40

LIFE WITH CHAINS

As it is with most industries—books, records, furniture—chain stores have taken over eyewear. The obvious advantages they have over the little guys (local opticians, and private ophthalmologists and optometrists who sell glasses) is that they are convenient— they offer numerous locations, and most offer same-day (if not one-hour) service; they have a huge selection of frames; and, for the most part, they charge less than private practitioners.

On the other hand, many people feel that they get a more thorough eye examination from a private ophthalmologist or optometrist. After all, if they're not linked with an optician, there's no motivation to recommend a new pair of glasses. And of course a private practitioner with whom you have developed

a relationship over the years will almost certainly give better advice than a big chain can.

In all, whether you go to a chain or a private office, don't leave until you've gotten exactly what you want. There's no reason to settle for less than meets the eye.

INSURE THINGS

Because glasses (and contact lenses) are often a major investment, it might be wise to have them insured against loss or destruction.

> " I was working in a cosmetics shop. A woman came in looking for something to bring out her bright blue eyes. I gave her meat skewers."
>
> HATTIE HAYRIDGE

SAFE SPECS

The American National Standards Institute (ANSI) has created three categories of sunglasses that indicate how much visible light, UVA, and UVB is allowed through the lenses. Beware of lenses that claim 100 percent UV protection, as this may refer to combined UVA and UVB protection.

COSMETIC

glasses are for everyday usage. They allow 60 percent of visible light through, and block 20 percent of UVA and 70 percent of UVB.

GENERAL PURPOSE

glasses are mainly for outdoor activities. They block between 60 and 92 percent of visible light, 60 percent of UVA, and at least 95 percent of UVB.

SPECIAL PURPOSE

glasses are designed for extremely bright situations such as skiing and block 97 percent of visible light, 60 percent of UVA, and at least 99 percent of UVB.

INTERNATIONAL SYMBOL FOR GLASSES REPAIR:

EYEGLASS REPAIR KIT

A portable kit for emergency repairs—the magnifying glass allows even the most nearsighted person a fair chance in replacing a missing hinge screw.

where.

A Chic Simple store looks out on the world beyond its shop window. Items are practical and comfortable and will work with pieces bought elsewhere. The store can be a cottage industry or a global chain, but even with an international vision it is still rooted in tradition, quality, and value.

FREEDOM OF CHOICE

Even as the world shrinks and chain stores expand globally, there are plenty of locales where choice is limited if there is any choice at all. However, most manufactueres today can aid you in finding a store or even mail direct to you. The U.S. numbers listed below will help give you freedom of choice.

Alain Mikli 800/829-8032

Anglo-American Eyewear 800/248-0199

Armani 800/344-6744

Bausch & Lomb Eyewear 800/828-1430

Calvin Klein 800/547-2020

Vuarnet 800/348-0388

DKNY 800/231-0884

Norma Kamali 800/852-6254

Ralph Lauren 800/775-7656

Revo 800/367-7386

Robert La Roche 800/851-5140

Serengeti 800/525-4001

MANUFACTURERS AND DISTRIBUTORS

Carrera Eyewear (distributor) 800/346-1734
*(Christian Dior, Hugo Boss, Carrera, Terry Brogan,
Alfred Dunhill, Porsche, Sun Jet, Christian Lacroix)*

Colors in Optics (distributor) 212/465-1200
(Perry Ellis, Kamali, Sting, Versace, b.u.m.)

Murai (distributor) 800/261-2268
*(Jean-Paul Gaultier, Julian Gaultier, Sonia Rykiel, Papa Hemmingway,
June July August, Murai Medel, Murai Cocoro)*

Optical Shop of Aspen (O.S.A.) (distributor) 800/647-2345
(Matsuda, Martine Sitbon, Takeo Kukuchi, Kansai, O.S.A.)

Optics Studio (distributor) 800/654-6099
(Pro Design, Gail Spence, Ticoline)

The Lantis Corporation (manufacturer) 800/551-1015
(Joseph Abboud, DKNY, Ray-Ban, Solargenics)

United States

ALABAMA

PARISIAN
2100 River Chase Galleria
Birmingham, AL 35244
205/987-4200 or
205/940-4000 for U.S. listings
(Sunglasses)

ARIZONA

FASHION EYE CENTER
6159 East Broadway
Tucson, AZ 85711
602/790-2020
(Designer eyewear)

OPTICAL EXPRESSIONS
2425 East Camelback Road,
Suite 106
Phoenix, AZ 85016
602/224-5772

OPTICAL SHOP OF
ASPEN
Biltmore Fashion Park
2522 East Camelback Road
Phoenix, AZ 85016
602/957-8033

PARIS OPTIQUE VIA
USA
8980 East Indian Bend Road,
Suite 1
Scottsdale, AZ 85250
602/951-0288
*(Designer prescription
eyeglasses and sunglasses; ship
anywhere in the world)*

RODIG OPTICAL
3822 East Fifth
Tucson, AZ 85716
602/325-9401
(Chic, unique eyewear)

ARKANSAS

ARKANSAS OPTICAL
COMPANY
1316 Main Street
North Little Rock, AR 72114
501/372-1923
*(Wide selection including
children's glasses and
designer frames)*

CALIFORNIA

ALAMEDA EYES
OPTOMETRY
1432 Park Street
Alameda, CA 94501
510/769-2020

CITY OPTIX
2154 Chestnut Street
San Francisco, CA 94123
415/921-1188

DR. LEVENTHAL'S
3680 Rosecrans
San Diego, CA 92110
619/223-2133
*(Sunglasses, contact lenses,
eyeglasses in an hour)*

EYES IN DISGUISE
2189 Union Street
San Francisco, CA 94123
415/474-5321

FIRST VISION
8851 Garden Grove
Boulevard, Suite 103
Garden Grove, CA 92644
714/530-9872

FRAME-N-LENS
15365 Freeway Drive
Santa Fe Springs, CA 90026
800/GLASSES for locations
in California

FRED SEGAL
8100 Melrose Avenue
Los Angeles, CA 90046
213/651-3342
(Sunglasses)

GIORGIO ARMANI
436 North Rodeo Drive
Beverly Hills, CA 90210
310/271-5555
(Designer eyewear)

INVISION
1907 Fillmore Street
San Francisco, CA 94115
415/563-9003

ITALEE OPTICAL
978 South Vermont Avenue
Los Angeles, CA 90006
213/385-1656

l.a. EYEWORKS
7407 Melrose Avenue
Los Angeles, CA 90046
213/653-8255
*(Carries full collection of l.a.
Eyeworks and exclusive
European and Japanese
collections)*

MAXFIELD
8825 Melrose Avenue
Los Angeles, CA 90069
310/274-8800
(Sunglasses)

MOSSIMO INC.
15320 Barranca
Irvine, CA 92718
714/453-1300
(Designer eyewear)

NEOSTYLE EYEWEAR
2605 State Street
San Diego, CA 92103
619/299-0755

THE OCULARIUM
2336 Chestnut Street
San Francisco, CA 94123
415/563-2475

OLIVER PEOPLES
8600 Sunset Boulevard
Los Angeles, CA 90069
310/657-5475

OPTICAL OUTLOOK
437-B North Bedford Drive
Beverly Hills, CA 90210
310/246-9468
(Custom-tailored eyewear)

REM OPTICAL
9301 Laurel Canyon
Boulevard
Arleta, CA 91331
818/504-3950
*(Converse, Rembrand, Daniel
Hunter, Esquire, REM line)*

RIMS + GOGGLES
3701 Sacramento Street
San Francisco, CA 94118
415/386-6866

SPECTACLES OF
UNION SQUARE
177 Maiden Lane
San Francisco, CA 94108
415/781-8556

WILLIAM LINDEN, O.D.
477 East Colorado Boulevard
Pasadena, CA 91101
818/796-1191
*(Lab on premises, with over
18 doctors on staff. Eyewear in
about an hour; open 7 days a
week)*

COLORADO

LAKESIDE VISION
CLINIC
5560 West 44th Avenue
Denver, CO 80212
303/421-2424
*(Eye exams and designer
eyewear)*

OPTICAL SHOP OF
ASPEN
308 Galena Street
Aspen, CO 81611
303/925-1525
(Specializes in sport optics)

CONNECTICUT

JOSEPH ABBOUD
325 Greenwich Avenue
Greenwich, CT 06830
203/869-2212
(Designer sunglasses)

DELAWARE

MCELHINNEY & KIRK,
INC.
Professional Building
Wilmington, DE 19803
302/652-3583
*(Selection of frames,
sunglasses, and sungoggles)*

DISTRICT OF
COLUMBIA

VOORTHUIS
OPTICIANS, INC
Mazza Gallerie
Washington, D.C. 20015
202/244-7114
*(Designer eyewear and
sunglasses)*

FLORIDA

AU COURANT OPTICAL
9700 Collins Avenue
101 Bal Harbour Shop
Bal Harbour, FL 33154
305/866-2020
(Designer eyewear)

COCO LUNETTE
3015 Grand Avenue
Coco Walk, Suite 178
Coconut Grove, FL 33133
305/441-0457
(Designer eyewear)

MR. I'S OPTICAL
5817 Sunset Drive
South Miami, FL 33143
305/661-1205
(Designer eyewear)

SUNGLASS HUT
INTERNATIONAL, INC.
120 S.W. 8th Street
Miami, FL 33130
800/597-5005 for U.S. and
international listings
*(Sunglasses, all-purpose
eyewear, and sports brands)*

GEORGIA

RICH'S
Lenox Square Shopping
Mall
3393 Peachtree Road
Atlanta, GA 30326
404/231-2611
(Sunglasses)

HAWAII

LIBERTY HOUSE
P.O. Box 2690
Ala Moana Shopping
Center
Honolulu, HI 96845
808/941-2345
(Sunglasses)

IDAHO

ROYAL OPTICAL
Hillcrest Shopping Center
Boise, ID 83705
208/343-1490
*(Wide selection, including
children's frames)*

ILLINOIS

THE OPTICAL SHOP
12 Merryville Professional
Center
Merryville, IL 62062
618/288-3550
*(Specializes in Varilux no-line
progressive lenses)*

VISUAL EFFECTS
OPTICAL
1953 North Clybourn
Chicago, IL 60614
312/281-0200

IOWA

PRECISE OPTICAL
FASHIONS
420 Pierce Street
Sioux City, IA 51101
712/252-3323
(Wide selection from basic to
designer frames)

MARYLAND

A & K OPTICAL
658 Kenilworth Drive,
Suite 202
Towson, MD 21204
410/823-8556

MCGINNIS OPTICIANS
3907 Branch Avenue
Temple Hills, MD 20748
301/423-1151
(Children's eyewear, sportwear
eyewear)

MASSACHUSETTS

JOSEPH ABBOUD
37 Newbury Street
Boston, MA 02116
617/266-4200
(Sunglasses, eyewear)

WELLESLEY OPTICAL
216 Newbury Street
Boston, MA 02116
617/247-2020

MICHIGAN

HERITAGE OPTICAL
6329 West Seven Mile Road
Detroit, MI 48221
313/863-9581
(High fashion frames)

OPTICAL FASHION
2801 West Big Beaver Road
Troy, MI 48084
313/643-6220
(High fashion frames)

MINNESOTA

SPECS
228 Hennepin Avenue
Minneapolis, MN 55405
612/374-2114

WHITEBEAR OPTICAL
4750 Washington Square
Whitebear Lake, MN 55110
612/429-5460

MONTANA

THE BENT LENS
23 West Main Street
Bozeman, MT 59715
406/586-4359
(Sunglasses, prescription
eyewear)

NEW JERSEY

EAGLE EYEWEAR INC.
P.O. Box 486
Whitehouse, NJ 08888
908/236-9300
(The John Lennon eyewear
collection)

PILDES OPTICAL
The Mall at Short Hills
JFK Parkway
Short Hills, NJ 07078
201/564-8520

SILHOUETTE EYEWEAR
266 Union Street
Northvale, NJ 07647
201/768-8600

SUPERSPECS FOR KIDS
ONLY
1178 Closter Plaza
Closter Shopping Center
Closter, NJ 07624
201/768-1717
(Frames and lenses for kids)

NEW MEXICO

CAROLINE STRANGE
OPTICIANS
201 Galisteo
Santa Fe, NM 87501
505/988-9510
(Designer eyewear)

EYEWORKS AT NOBHILL
3411 Central N.E.
Albuquerque, NM 87106
505/254-1300

NEW YORK

MARCHON EYEWEAR
35 Hub Drive
Melville, NY 11747
516/755-2020 or
800/645-1300
(Disney children's eyewear and
adult designer glasses)

PERRY ELLIS EYEWEAR
DESIGN
136 Oak Drive
Syosset, NY 11791
516/364-3664
(Perry Ellis, Pierre Cardin,
Elizabeth Arden, and Bonjour
eyewear)

New York City

ALAIN MIKLI
880 Madison Avenue
New York, NY 10021
212/633-0777
(Designer eyewear handmade in
France)

GRUEN OPTIKA
1225 Lexington Avenue
New York, NY 10028
212/628-2493
(Frames and lenses for adults
and children)

H.L. PURDY OPTICIAN
501 Madison Avenue
New York, NY 10022
212/688-8050

JOEL NAME
65 West Houston Street
New York, NY 10012
212/777-5888
(French line of eyewear)

KIMBE
430 Park Avenue
New York, NY 10022
212/838-5522
(Designer eyewear)

LAYTONS OPTICAL
130 East 59th Street
New York, NY 10022
212/755-0498

LUGENE
987 Madison Avenue
New York, NY 10021
212/717-4885
(Designer eyewear)

MATSUDA
461 Park Avenue
New York, NY 10022
212/935-6969
(Sunglasses)

MORGENTHAL
FREDERICS
OPTICIANS
944 Madison Avenue
New York, NY 10021
212/744-9444

MYOPTICS
42 St. Marks Place
New York, NY 10003
212/533-1577
(Eye exams, vintage and
designer frames)

OPTIC ZONE
220 Columbus Avenue
New York, NY 10023
212/724-5450

OPTICAL AFFAIRS
INC.
5–9 Union Square West,
6th floor
New York, NY 10003
212/727-3080
(Christian Roth eyewear)

OUTER VISION
1400 Broadway
New York, NY 10018
212/221-4595

PARAGON SPORTING
GOODS
867 Broadway
New York, NY 10003
212/255-8036
(Sports eyewear, sunglasses)

PAUL SMITH
108 Fifth Avenue
New York, NY 10011
212/627-9770
(Sunglasses)

PILDES OPTICAL
2261 Broadway
New York, NY 10024
212/877-2980

ROBERT LA ROCHE
OF AMERICA
11 Penn Plaza
New York, NY 10001
212/279-1002

ROBERT MARC
OPTICIANS
782 Madison Avenue
New York, NY 10021
212/737-6000

SELIMA OPTIC
59 Wooster Street
New York, NY 10012
212/343-9490
(Designer frames, 30s–60s
vintage frames)

SOLARGENICS
461 Fifth Avenue
New York, NY 10017
212/686-1500

NORTH CAROLINA

MECKLENBURG
OPTICAL
2015 Randolph Road #106
Charlotte, NC 28207
704/333-3384

OHIO

OPTICAL ARTS
2934 West Central 06
Toledo, OH 43606
419/535-7837
(Fashion eyewear with
personalized frames)

TUCKERMAN OPTICAL
64 East Broad Street
Columbus, OH 43215
614/221-0515

OREGON

BINYON'S
12000 S.E. 82nd Avenue
Portland, OR 97266
503/659-5947
(Wide selection from basic to
designer frames, sports and
children's frames)

SEEING IS BELIEVING
908 N.W. 23rd Avenue
Portland, OR 97210
503/221-1459

PENNSYLVANIA

EYEGLASS
ENCOUNTERS
1937 Chestnut Street
Philadelphia, PA 19103
215/854-0441
(Designer eyewear and
sunglasses, specializes in
hard-to-fit contact lenses)

THE EYEGLASS WORKS
4407 Main Street
Philadelphia, PA 19127
215/487-2711

FABULOUS FANNY'S
112 1/2 North 6th Street
Allentown, PA 18101
215/432-1826
(Antique frames and optical
accessories)

SQUIRREL EYETIQUE
2242 Murray Avenue
Pittsburgh, PA 15217
412/422-5300

WEST COAST OPTICAL
1701 Chestnut Street
Philadelphia, PA 19103
215/977-8555
*(High-end designer and
economical eyewear)*

TEXAS

AMERICAN EYEWEAR
8309 Preston Road
Dallas, TX 75225
214/750-5793

EYE ELEGANCE
1800 Postal Boulevard
Houston, TX 77056
713/622-4411

THE OPTICAL
CORPORATION OF
AMERICA
3410 Midcourt
Carrollton, TX 75006
214/702-3600

WASHINGTON

ELEGANT EYE
1661 East Olive Way
Seattle, WA 98102
206/322-2020

NATIONAL LISTINGS AND CHAINS

AMERICAN VISION
CENTER
90 John Street
New York, NY 10038
800/232-5558 for U.S.
listings

BARNEYS NEW YORK
106 Seventh Avenue
New York, NY 10011
212/929-9000 or
800/777-0087 for
U.S. listings
(Sunglasses)

BERGDORF GOODMAN
754 Fifth Avenue
New York, NY 10019
212/753-7300
*(Upscale department store,
sunglasses)*

BLOOMINGDALE'S
1000 Third Avenue
New York, NY 10022
212/355-5900 for
U.S. listings
(Sunglasses)

DAYTON'S
MARSHALL FIELD
700 On the Mall
Minneapolis, MN 55402
612/375-2200
(Sunglasses)

EASTERN MOUNTAIN
SPORTS
1 Vose Farm Road
Peterborough, NH 03458
603/924-7231
*(Topo® sunglasses for
mountaineering/hiking)*

EDDIE BAUER
1330 Fifth and Union
Seattle, WA 98101
206/622-2766
800/426-8020 for catalogue
(Sunglasses)

EMPORIO ARMANI
110 Fifth Avenue
New York, NY 10011
212/727-3240 or
212/570-1122 for
international listings
(Armani eyewear)

FOR EYES OPTICAL
285 West 74th Place
Hialeah, FL 33014
800/367-1026
(Chain)

GALERIES LAFAYETTE
10 East 57th Street
Trump Tower
New York, NY 10022
212/355-0022
*(Upscale department store,
sunglasses)*

LENSCRAFTERS
INTERNATIONAL
8650 Governors Hill Drive
Cincinatti, OH 45249
513/583-6000 or
800/522-LENS for
international listings

NEIMAN MARCUS
1618 Main Street
Dallas, TX 75201
210/573-5780
*(Upscale department store,
sunglasses)*

NORDSTROM
1501 Fifth Avenue
Seattle, WA 98191
206/628-2111
*(Upscale department store,
sunglasses)*

OPTI-WORLD
1820 The Exchange,
Suite 405
Atlanta, GA 33039
404/916-2020
(Chain)

PEARLEVISION
2534 Royal Lane
Dallas, TX 75229
214/277-5000 or
800/YES-EYES for
international listings

POLO/RALPH LAUREN
EYEWEAR
867 Madison Avenue
New York, NY 10021
212/606-2100 for
U.S. listings
(Designer eyewear)

PRICE CLUB
P.O. Box 85466
San Diego, CA 92186
619/581-4600 for
West Coast listings
703/406-6800 for
East Coast listings
(Chain)

R.E.I.
1525 11th Avenue
Seattle, WA 98122
800/426-4840 for national
store listings and catalogue
*(Activewear and outdoor
recreational gear)*

R.H. MACY & CO.
(Bullock's, I. Magnin,
Aéropostale)
Macy's Herald Square
151 West 34th Street
New York, NY 10011
212/695-4400 for
East Coast listings
415/393-3457 for
West Coast listings
(Department store)

SAKS FIFTH AVENUE
611 Fifth Avenue
New York, NY 10022
212/753-4000 for
U.S. listings
(Sunglasses)

URBAN OUTFITTERS
1801 Walnut Street
Philadelphia, PA 19103
215/569-3131
215/564-2313 for
U.S. listings
(Sunglasses)

VISIONWORKS
8333 Bryar Dairy Road
Largo, FL 34647
800/399-6000
(Chain)

INTERNATIONAL
LISTINGS

Australia

MELBOURNE

DAIMARU
211 La Trobe Street
3/660-6666
*(Upscale department store,
sunglasses)*

Canada

MONTREAL

LES BÉSICLES
3511 Boulevard Saint-
Laurent
514/982-6030
(Designer frames)

HARRY TOULCH
4021 St. Lawrence Boulevard
514/849-1433
(Designer eyewear)

HOLT RENFREW
1300 rue Sherbrooke Ouest
514/842-5111
(Department store, sunglasses)

OGILVY
1307 rue Sainte-Catherine
Ouest
514/842-7711
(Sunglasses)

TORONTO

FIRST CANADIAN
OPTICAL
P.O. Box 261
First Canadian Place
M5X 1C8
(Designer eyewear)

France

AVIGNON

OPTIQUE LAVAL
SIMONNET
26, rue de la République
84000
90/86-12-85

GRENOBLE

OPTIQUE BOURGAREL
2, place de l'Étoile
38000
76/43-02-72

LIMOGES

OPTIQUE LASCAUX
2, place Denis-Dussoubs
84000
55/77-79-40

PARIS

ALAIN MIKLI
1, rue des Rosiers
75004
42/72-01-56
(Frames and lenses)

IL POUR L'HOMME
209, rue Saint-Honoré
75001
42/60-43-56
(Sunglasses)

JEAN LOUIS FOUCALET
13, place Adolphe-Cherioux
75015
45/33-95-55

L.V.T.
13, boulevard Raspail
75007

LAFONT & FILS
OPTIQUE
1, rue Duphot
75001
42/60-01-02

MIKI PARIS OPTIQUE
33, avenue de l'Opéra
75002
42/61-72-48
*(Staff will re-color lenses on
rush orders and deliver)*

OPTIC BASTILLE
38, rue de la Roquette
75011
48/06-87-00
(hip and eccentric styles)

OPTIQUE DE LA
PLAINE MONCEAU
78, rue de Villiers
75017
47/63-60-97

OPTIQUE DES
ENTREPRENEURS
39, rue des Entrepreneurs
75015
45/78-03-61

Germany

BAYREUTH

HEUBERGER OPTIK
Maximilienstrasse 7
95444
921/653-63

BERLIN

BRILLE
Kurfürstendamm 54
10707
30/882-6696
(Designer eyewear)

UNI OPTIK
Knesebeckstrasse 6/7
10623
30/312-9017

DÜSSELDORF

OPTICAL AFFAIRS
GMBH
Verdingerstrasse 12
40474
211/470-8091
*(Handmade eyewear designed
by Christian Roth)*

ERLANGEN

AMBERG OPTIK
Hauptstrasse 24
91054
9131/211-62

HAMBURG

FIELMANN OPTIK
Weidestrasse 118A
22083
40/270-760

LUDWIGSBURG

HUNKE OPTIK
Kirchstrasse 19
71634
7141/926-875

MUNICH

FIELMANN OPTIK
Sonnenstrasse 1
80331
89/593-108

Great Britain

LONDON

BOOTS OPTICIANS
602/49-3786 for
U.K. listings

CHATOO & CO. LTD.
258 Kensington High Street
W8
71/602-3065
*(Optometrists, designer frames
and spectacles, contact lenses)*

CUTLER & GROSS
16 Knightsbridge Garden
SW1
71/581-2250
(Sunglasses and spectacles)

DAVID CLULOW
OPTICIANS
82 Kensington High Street
W8
71/937-1984
*(Ophthalmic opticians,
designer frames and spectacles,
contact lenses)*

DOLLAND AND
AITCHISON
127a Sloane Street
SW1
71/730-4870
*(Brand-name frames as well as
own design; ophthalmic
opticians)*

EYE-TECH LTD.
33 King's Road
SW3
71/730-1188
*(Opticians, designer frames,
contact lenses)*

HACKETT CLOTHIERS
136–138 Sloane Street
NW
71/730-3331

HARRODS
87–135 Brompton Road
SW1
71/730-1234
(Sunglasses)

LILLYWHITES LTD.
24–30 Regent Street
Piccadilly Circus SW1
71/915-4000
(For sports eyewear)

PAUL SMITH LTD.
41–44 Floral Street
WC23 9DJ
71/379-7133 or
212/627-9770 for
worldwide info
(Sunglasses)

THE SPECTACLE SHOP
44 Theobalds Road
WC1
71/938-1251
(Can make lenses for any
frame)

Italy

MILAN

COIN
Piazza Cinque Giornateo
(Selection of sunglasses)

ISTITUTO OTTICO
VITANO
Corso Matteotti, 22
2/76-00-01-00
(Sunglasses, frames, lenses)

OTTICA SAN CARLO
Galleria Passarella, 2
2/79-88-27
(Sunglasses, frames, lenses)

LA RINASCENTE
Piazza del Duomo
2/88-521
(Selection of sunglasses)

Japan

TOKYO

HAKUSAN
Shibuya Parco #3 Bldg. 2F
14–15 Udagawa

Shibuya-ku
3/3477-5926
(Fine designer glasses)

LUNEETTA BADA
Vivre Bldg. 3F
5-10-1 Jingu-mae
Shibuya-ku
3/3499-3119
(Contemporary designer
glasses)

OPTICIEN LOYD
4-26-35 Jingu-mae
Shibuya-ku
3/3423-0505
(Original designs and imported
glasses)

OGURA CO. LTD
Momose Bldg. 7F
1-24-4 Shibuya, Shibuya-ku
150
3/5466-1956

TAKASHIMAYA
2-4-1 Nihonbashi
Chuo-ku
3/3211-4111

RESOURCES

JACKET FRONT

    Wraparound sunglasses, Ray Ban

BACK

    (from top) Plastic "eye cups," H.L. Purdy Opticians; Antique welding glasses, Robert Warner collection; Modern welding protective eyewear, Canal Street, NYC

SPECTACLES

10 **BLUE TINTED GLASSES** (above) Steel "Maxi" sunglasses, Jeffrey Miller collection; (below) 19th-c. wire frames, Edward Welch, Winslow, ME

17 **PROTECTIVE** (from top) Plastic "eye cups," H.L. Purdy Opticians; Antique welding glasses, Robert Warner collection; Modern welding protective eyewear, Canal Street, NYC

22-23 **STYLE** Modern cat's-eye with aluminum frame and plastic arms, Martine Sitbon at Robert Marc, NYC

ANATOMY

26 Tortoiseshell hand-held monocle/magnifier, Robert Marc, NYC

31 Two pairs of clip-on sunglasses, Khi Ban collection by Robert La Roche

32 (clockwise from upper left) **BRIDGE** Epoxy frame by l.a. Eyeworks; **TEMPLE** (top to bottom) Straight black library temple, Jeffrey Miller collection; Cable temple, Anglo-American Eyewear; Regular temple, Romeo Gigli; **NOSE-PIECE** "Wireless" frames by Bada, Robert Marc Opticians; **HINGES** (left to right) Vintage gold-toned frame, Quality Vision Eye Center; Aluminum frame, Riviera

34 **SIMPLE GLASSES** Vintage wireless glasses, Edward Welch, Winslow, ME

36-37 Assorted **CLIP-ONS** from Anglo-American Eyewear, l.a. Eyeworks, Oliver Peoples, Pro Design, Robert La Roche

38 **CASES** (clockwise from upper left) Aluminum case, Oliver Peoples; Leather cigar-case style, Robert Marc; Vintage faux crocodile, Jeffrey Miller collection; Punched leather, Morgenthal Frederics; Basketweave aluminum, Selima, Soho; Brushed aluminum, Oliver Peoples; Synthetic suede (ultra suede), Vuarnet; Black lizard by Opti Etui, Morgenthal Frederics; Leather cigar-case style, Robert Marc

39 Metal half-glasses with "slider" temples, Oliver Peoples; Polishing cloths, Oliver Peoples

VISUAL LEXICON

42 **READING GLASSES** Collapsible metal reading glasses, H.L. Purdy Opticians

44-45 **READING GLASSES** (left to right) Titanium and plastic half-glasses, Jan Houmard for Pro Design; Metal half-frames, Calvin Klein at H.L. Purdy Opticians; Brushed metal, Anglo-American Eyewear; The Zina frame, Lugene; Wire frame, Anglo-American Eyewear; Tortoiseshell half-glasses, Lens Crafters; "Scroll" frames, Jean Lafont; Half-sunglasses, Sting for Colors in Optics; Rhinestone-trimmed plastic, Emmanuelle Khanh at H.L. Purdy Opticians; "Lifesaver" half-glasses, Morgenthal Frederics

48 **WIRE RIMS** (left to right) Metal frames, Giorgio Armani Occhiali from H.L. Purdy Opticians; Early reading glasses, Edward Welch, Winslow, ME

49 **WIRE RIMS** (from top) Black metal, Ralph Lauren at H.L. Purdy Opticians; 19th-c. wire rims, Fabulous Fanny's, Allentown, PA; Gold metal, DKNY; Silver metal sunglasses, Issey Miyake at Robert Marc Opticians; Copper wire rims, Red Rose at H.L. Purdy Opticians

50 **TORTOISESHELL** Plastic tortoiseshell frames, a selection from Morgenthal Frederics, Robert Marc, Colors in Optics, Robert La Roche, Alain Mikli, Giorgio Armani, Eyevan, and Joseph Abboud

52 **TORTOISESHELL** (clockwise from top) Full-circle, Anglo-American Eyewear; "Lifesaver," Morgenthal Frederics; Celluloid driving spectacles c. 1920, Stanton Blackmer collection; Randomly spotted plastic, Anglo-American Eyewear; Rectangular frames, Ichi•Ban, Robert La Roche; The Oberlin frame and plastic chain, Morgenthal Frederics

53 **TORTOISESHELL** (clockwise from upper left) Plastic case, Oliver Peoples; Oval plastic tortoise and metal frames, Oliver Peoples; Cat's-eye sunglass, Cutler & Gross of London; Vintage child's cat's-eye frames, Robert Warner collection; Handmade classics, Robert Marc; Septi-lateral frame, Robert La Roche; Vintage "owl-eyes" sunglasses, Jeffrey Miller collection

54 **HORN-RIMS** Military issue, James Wojcik collection

56 **HORN-RIMS** (clockwise from upper left) Folding vintage cat's-eye sunglasses, Jeffrey Miller collection; Handmade bamboo-colored horn-rims, Hakusan at Robert Marc Opticians; The Cary Grant frame, Oliver Peoples; Vintage olive-colored horn-rims, Quality Vision Eye Center, New York; Classic black reading glasses by DKNY

57 **HORN-RIMS** (clockwise from upper left) Romeo Gigli horn and wire rims, H.L. Purdy Opticians; "Secret Agent" sunglasses, Jeffrey Miller collection; Round "Corbusier" frames, Robert Warner collection; Hand-held lorgnette, Robert Marc Opticians; Wood-grained patterned horn rim, 26th Street flea market, NYC; Classic horn-rims, Anglo-American eyewear

58 Variety of **VINTAGE CAT'S-EYE** frames, Robert Warner collection

60 **TINTS** (from left) Circular half-toned tinted glasses, Cutler & Gross, London; Cherry red sunglasses, Christian Roth Optical Affairs; Round glasses with clip-on sunshades, Anglo-American Eyewear; Half-toned spectacles by Claude Montana, Lauren Shakely collection

61 **TINTS** (from top) Children's frames, Jean Lafont; The Omar frame, metallic with clip-ons, l.a. Eyeworks; Blue plastic frames (with metal arms), Claude Montana for Alain Mikli; Plastic "Rainbow" oval frames, Anglo-American Eyewear; Silver metal, Christian Roth, Optical Affairs

63 **METAL FRAMES** (from top) Chrome frame, Junior Gaultier; Rope frame sunglasses by Christian Roth, Optical Affairs; Baroque cat's-eye sunglasses, l.a. Eyeworks; Round steel frames, vintage collection, Quality Vision Eye Center; "Eyebrow" frame, DKNY

SPORT GLASSES

64 **SNORKELING MASK** from Paragon Sporting Goods

66 (upper right) **RAY-BAN**, (lower left) **AVIATOR**, both from Bausch & Lomb

67 (upper right) **WAYFARER**; (lower left) **ARMY-NAVY**

68 **MIRRORED** (top) Maxi oval frames, Cutler & Gross, London; (middle left) Wire frames, Cutler & Gross, London; (middle right) Wire rim sunglasses, Norma Kamali for Colors in Optics; (bottom) Classic aviators, Ray-Ban

71 **SPORT** Vintage 80s knock-off of classic early-70s protective, reflective Olympic ski eyewear, Jeffrey Miller collection

72 **AERODYNAMIC** (from top) Mumbos Frame in gray by Oakley, Paragon; Eyeshade by Oakley, Paragon; Sport glasses, Vuarnet

73 **AERODYNAMIC** Bronzed-toned mirrored sports glasses by Gargoyles USA

74 **MOUNTAIN SPORTS** (from top) Snowboard strap, Chums, Paragon; "Plunge" with orange lens, Nikon; Glacier glasses with amber lens, nose and side shield, and red croakie strap, Topo Optics from EMS; Mountaineer with reflective lens, side shield, and elastic strap, Vuarnet

76 **PROTECTIVE** (from top) Racquetball safety glasses by Leader, Paragon Sporting Goods; Vintage steel motorcycle safety glasses, Robert Warner collection; Leather and steel tie-on driving glasses c. 1920s, Edward Welch, Winslow, ME; Two examples, in clear and black, of basketball safety glasses, NBA Eyewear

77 **CROAKIES** (left) Tortiseshell Wayfarer II sunglasses by Bausch & Lomb, with standard black croakies, Paragon; (right) Chums, The Original Eyewear Retainer, Paragon

79 **SPECIALTY** (from top) The Allen ski shield lens mask by Bollé, H.L. Purdy Opticians; Motorcycle goggles by Halcyon, courtesy of James Wojcik; The Genesis face mask by Sherwood, Paragon; Profocus corrective lens swim goggles by Speedo, Paragon

QUOTES

2 **JIMMY DURANTE,** *The Penguin Book of Modern Humorous Quotations* (Penguin, 1987).

11 **RALPH WALDO EMERSON,** *Journals,* 1863 (International Thesaurus of Quotations).

13 **MARLON BRANDO,** *21st Century Dictionary of Quotations* (Dell, 1993).

20 **GARRY SHANDLING,** *1,911 Best Things Anybody Ever Said* (Random House, 1988).

24 **FRED ALLEN,** *The Penguin Book of Modern Humorous Quotations* (Penguin, 1987).

27 **JONATHAN SWIFT,** *Correct Quotes,* Portions by Donald L. Smith, Jon Winokur (Word Star International, 1992).

35 **KIT HOLLERBACH,** *Just Joking,* Portions by Career Publishing, Inc. (Word Star International, 1992).

41 **STEVEN WRIGHT,** *The Montreal Comedy Fest Juste Pur Rire* (Performance, 1989).

48 **WINSTON CHURCHILL,** *Correct Quotes,* Portions by Career Publishing, Inc. (Word Star International, 1992).

55 **P. J. O'ROURKE,** *Modern Manners* (Dell, 1983).

62 **HENRY MORGAN,** Song title, *Just Joking,* Portions by Donald L. Smith, Jon Winokur (Word Star International, 1992).

65 **JULES TANNEN,** *Just Joking,* Portions by Donald L. Smith, Jon Winokur (Word Star International, 1992).

67 **FRAN LEBOWITZ,** *original.*

70 **LEO DUROCHER,** *Speaking of Baseball,* edited by David Plant (Running Press, 1993).

82 **HATTIE HAYRIDGE,** *Just Joking,* Portions by Donald L. Smith, Jon Winokur (Word Star International, 1992).

104 **GEORGE MEREDITH,** *The Ordeal of Richard Feverel,* 1859 (International Thesaurus of Quotations).

ACKNOWLEDGMENTS

MANUFACTURER & RETAIL RESEARCH
Jeannette Durkan

QUOTE RESEARCH
Lige Rushing & Kate Doyle Hooper

ORIGINAL INTERVIEWS
Cynthia Stuart

AND SPECIAL THANKS TO: The American Optometric Association, Willy Barth, Sherryl Betesh, Tony Chirico, M. Scott Cookson, Lauri Del Commune, Chris DiMaggio, Michael Drazen, Borden Elniff, Jane Friedman, Janice Goldklang, Jo-Anne Harrison, Patrick Higgins, Katherine Hourigan, Dina Dell'Arciprete-Houser, Andy Hughes, Carol Janeway, Barbara Jones-Diggs, Nicholas Latimer, William Loverd, Anne McCormick, Dwyer McIntosh, Sonny Mehta, Lan Nguyen, Mitchell Rosenbaum, Lauren Shakely, Anne-Lise Spitzer, Meg Stebbins, Robin Swados, Robert Takacs, Aileen Tse, Vision Council of America, Katherine Wallach, Shelley Wanger, Robert Warner, Edward Welch, Wayne Wolf.

COMMUNICATIONS

The world has gotten smaller and faster but we still can only be in one place at a time, which is why we are anxious to hear from you. We would like your input on stores and products that have impressed you. We are always happy to answer any questions you have about items in the book, and of course we are interested in feedback about Chic Simple.

Our address is:
84 WOOSTER STREET
NEW YORK, NY 10012
PHONE (212) 343-9677 • FAX (212) 343-9678
email address: **info@chicsimple.com**
compuserve number **72704,2346**

Stay in touch because "The more you know, the less you need."

KIM JOHNSON GROSS & JEFF STONE

COLOPHON

TYPE

The text of this book was set in two typefaces: New Baskerville and Futura. The ITC version of **NEW BASKERVILLE** is called Baskerville, which itself is a facsimile reproduction of types cast from molds made by John Baskerville (1706–1775) from his designs. Baskerville's original face was one of the forerunners of the typestyle known to printers as the "modern face"—a "modern" of the period A.D. 1800. **FUTURA** was produced in 1928 by Paul Renner (1878–1956), former director of the Munich School of Design, for the Bauer Type Foundry. Futura is simple in design and wonderfully restful in reading. It has been widely used in advertising because of its even, modern appearance in mass and its harmony with a great variety of other modern types.

SEPARATION AND FILM PREPARATION BY

DIGITAL PRE-PRESS, INC.
New York, New York

PRINTED AND BOUND BY

FRIESEN PRINTERS
Altona, Manitoba, Canada

HARDWARE

Apple Macintosh Quadra 700 personal computers; APS Technologies Syquest Drives; Radius Precision Color Display/20; Radius 24X series Video Board; Hewlett Packard LaserJet 4, Supra Fax Modem

SOFTWARE

QuarkXPress 3.11, Adobe Photoshop 2.5.1, Microsoft Word 5.1

MUSICWARE

Pearl Jam, Daniel Lanois (*For the Beauty of Wynona*), Declaration of Independents (*Part 2*), Lyle Lovett (*Joshua Judges Ruth*), Holly Cole Trio (*Don't Smoke in Bed*), Steve Forbert (*The American in Me*), Björk (*Debut*), Prudence (*Songs of Greg Brown*), Chris Isaak (*San Francisco Days*), REM (*Eponymous*), Cole Porter (*Night and Day*), Cowboy Junkies (*The Trinity Session*), Eric Clapton (*Crossroads*), Bob Marley (*Legend*), Neil Young and Crazy Horse (*Weld*), Assorted Artists (*Love Gets Strange—The Songs of John Hiatt*), Julee Cruise (*The Voice of Love*), Smashing Pumpkins (*Siamese Twins*), Gavin Bryars (*Jesus's Blood Never Failed Me Yet*), Jimmie Dale Gilmore (*Spinning Around the Sun*), US 3 (*Hand on the Torch*)

Special thanks to Cathy O'Brien of Capitol Records, Inc.

"Perfect simplicity is unconsciously audacious."

GEORGE MEREDITH

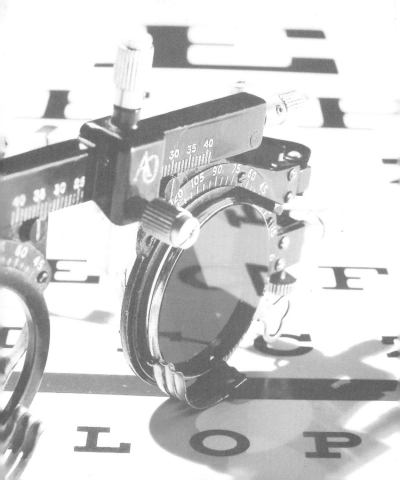